Focus on LinkedIn
Create a Personal Brand on LinkedIn™ to Make
More Money, Generate Leads, and Find
Employment

Richard G Lowe, Jr

Focus on LinkedIn
Create a Personal Brand on LinkedIn™ to Make More
Money, Generate Leads, and Find Employment

Business Professional Series #7

Published by The Writing King
www.thewritingking.com

Focus on LinkedIn™

Cover Artist: *theamateurzone*

ASIN: B01CX3B8GG
ISBN: 978-1-943517-21-3 (Paperback)
ISBN: 978-1-943517-62-6 (Hardcover)
ISBN: 978-1-943517-20-6 (eBook)

Library of Congress Control Number: 2016901777

Table of Contents

Introduction

"Brand is not a product, that's for sure; it's not one item. It's an idea, it's a theory, it's a meaning, it's how you carry yourself. It's aspirational; it's inspirational." — **Kevin Plank**

Would you like to build a network of people who are like-minded and responsive to your message? Do you want to receive qualified leads day after day? Are you confused about how to use LinkedIn to get your message out or to generate new business? Did you create a LinkedIn profile, only to have it just sit there and collect virtual dust?

Read this book to get the answers to all of those questions and more. You'll learn how to use LinkedIn as your primary professional social media platform and how to leverage your social networking reach. By the time you've completed reading, you will gain an understanding of where LinkedIn fits into your marketing campaigns and your professional life.

Used correctly, LinkedIn is an incredibly powerful professional networking tool which can get your brand and message delivered directly to a target audience of business professionals. A well-written profile which is kept up-to-date can generate leads for new business, improve your image to your customers and fellow professionals, and help you find employment.

Unlike other social media platforms, LinkedIn is intended to be used for business and professional activities. Do not confuse LinkedIn with other social networking sites; save your personal, political or similar commentary for Google+, Facebook or similar networks.

The idea behind *Focus On LinkedIn* is to show you how to use LinkedIn as the focus of your professional brand. There are many other books and courses on how to market using LinkedIn, how to generate leads, and how to optimize your profile. Those books will complement the information within this volume.

Does LinkedIn work? I receive well-qualified leads regularly, and these have resulted in quite a bit of new business. In fact, I have acquired more business through LinkedIn than via any other marketing effort.

It is important that your profile communicates your message in a manner which is easy to understand. Doing this helps people find out more about you, your business, and your products and services.

Using LinkedIn to define your personal brand requires time and effort; if you need help creating an excellent profile, the services from LinkedIn Makeover can help. We specialize in creating optimal LinkedIn profiles for business professionals. In my role as a **Senior Branding Consultant**, I work with executives, managers and others all over the world to ensure that their profile portrays their brand persuasively.

Before doing anything with LinkedIn, complete your profile, regardless of whether you write it yourself or contract with a company such as LinkedIn Makeover to compose it for you. Use the summary to define your brand and your message, while the remaining sections

— experiences, education, and so forth — reinforce your depth of experience and knowledge.

Once you've completed your profile, you can begin to leverage the power of LinkedIn. Creating the perfect profile isn't enough to promote your brand, although it's a great start. To put yourself out there in front of people – to gain their eyeballs so to speak – you have to communicate with them on a regular basis.

In other words, it's all about building relationships with your customers, coworkers, peers, managers, vendors, consultants and others; the people whom you want to be interested in your business, products, and services.

The purpose of this book is to help guide you through the maze of LinkedIn, so you can use it effectively in your professional and business life. Doing so will result in an extensive network of professionals becoming interested in you, your products and your services, and potentially lead to increased income.

What this Book is Not

The LinkedIn help system is very thorough and contains a large amount of information that is useful in explaining many of its features. For that reason, this book does not go into detail on the steps for each thing you can do with LinkedIn. In some cases, to make it easier, I've included a direct link to the appropriate LinkedIn help page with explanations of how to perform a task.

Additionally, there are many books and online articles containing tutorials and detailed information about every possible feature of LinkedIn. This book will tell you the best way to make use of each of the entries within LinkedIn to communicate your personal brand and build your network; look in the LinkedIn help system, online tutorials, or other books for detailed instructions on how to implement and use each feature.

With any large, web-based applications such as LinkedIn, changes are always occurring. LinkedIn hires a vast number of developers, designers, and testers which modify existing features, remove some functions, and add new ones all the time.

Because of this, some of the instructions or screenshots may not exactly match what you see when you log into LinkedIn.

Enjoy the Book

I hope you enjoy what I've written and find it to be of some value. If you would like to send me a note about this book, feel free to write me at *rich@thewritingking.com*. If you enjoyed the book, please write a *positive review on Amazon*.

Personal Branding

"Regardless of age, regardless of position, regardless of the business we happen to be in, all of us need to understand the importance of branding. We are CEOs of our own companies: ME Inc. To be in business today our most important job is to be head marketer for the brand called YOU." – **Tom Peters, Author, In Search of Excellence**

Have you often wondered why employers are not returning your calls? Have you been interviewed but have not received any offers? Are your efforts at selling your services falling flat?

Does this cause you to wonder what the hell is wrong with you?

There is probably nothing wrong with you at all; it could be that the image you are portraying on the Internet is hindering your efforts to sell your products and services or gain employment.

In other words, the personal brand or image illustrated by information, photos and videos that you posted on the internet is not presenting you in a positive light. In fact, this information is likely to be undermining your attempts to sell or find employment.

"Personal branding is about managing your name — even if you don't own a business — in a world of misinformation, disinformation, and semi-permanent Google records. Going on a date? The chances are that your "blind" date has Googled your name. Going to a job interview? Ditto." – **Tim Ferriss, Author, The 4-Hour Workweek**

What is a personal brand? It is how the world perceives you and the impression that you create in the minds of other people. In the physical world, you are judged by your attire, cleanliness, intelligence, skills, experience and other attributes. These are the impressions that people gain from you using sight, smell, intuition, and so forth.

The concept of personal branding carries over into the virtual world of the Internet. Information posted on your social media, blogs, websites or other publicly available places on the web creates a picture of you in the minds of viewers.

For example, if there are hundreds of pictures of you on social media sites such as Facebook getting drunk, partying, and throwing up, then you have created an impression of a drunken alcoholic with everything that implies. That's not a very professional personal brand, and it may make it challenging for you to get hired, attract clients, or even get involved in a meaningful relationship.

During my career, I've hired several hundred employees and consultants, performed interviews with hundreds more potential employees and examined thousands upon thousands of resumes. In the days before the Internet, I depended upon reference calls, employment agencies, resumes, and background checks to find out more about a candidate and to validate their information.

In the last few years, however, I came to depend more and more on the Internet, because of the vast amount of information that could be found out about a person with a few simple searches. It's amazing, and a little bit frightening, just how much is available online for anyone to see.

It is astonishing how much of this information is negative or unflattering. Even more interesting is that the photos, videos, and other media were put online by the individuals themselves. So many people are afraid of what the government or big corporations may find out about them, and yet those same people routinely slander themselves online.

It's imperative that you take an active role in maintaining your online image. If you're like most people you frequently use Facebook or other social networks to post pictures, videos, and updates on a regular basis. It's a good idea to audit your social network accounts on a regular basis and delete anything that doesn't show you in a positive light.

You can be sure that your boss, your children, significant other, friends, family, customers, employees, and suppliers will search for you and examine whatever is there to see. Unflattering information can even make it difficult to purchase insurance, get a loan, buy a house, or rent an apartment.

The worst part is that information that you have posted yourself is, naturally, considered credible. After all, why would anyone post false information about themselves?

On a professional level, your LinkedIn profile is arguably the most important social network and as such it should be the focus of your personal branding journey. When I used the Internet to research a potential hire (whether an employee or consultant), I began my search with LinkedIn. I could tell a lot about a person by the state of their LinkedIn profile. A sloppy or hastily put together one earned a negative mark, and grammar or spelling errors even more so.

Conversely, a well thought out, polished profile reinforced their positive image. A good write-up gives enough information to learn about a person's professional qualifications and gain some insight into their knowledge, skills, experiences and how they might fit into the organization. The completeness, correctness, and thoroughness of their online summary communicates quite a bit about their professional stature and image.

This book is specifically about LinkedIn and how to use it to create a personal, professional brand. As with all journeys, there is a beginning, and LinkedIn, since it focuses on the professional, is a great place to begin your branding journey.

It is by no means the end, as there are other social networks as well as blogs, websites, and many other places where information about you is available to the general public. Once you have your LinkedIn correctly written, you should make it a part of your branding effort to audit, modify and even delete anything else out that you can control.

Quite often there is information on the Internet that you can't change for various reasons. But you can ensure that everything you can control portrays you in a positive and useful light. In fact, not doing so will harm you and tarnish your reputation.

Focus on LinkedIn

"Your LinkedIn profile must be consistent with how you portray yourself elsewhere. Not only should your official résumé match the experience you list on LinkedIn, but it also should be consistent with Twitter and public Facebook information." — **Melanie Pinola, Author, LinkedIn in 30 Minutes**

What's the best way to take advantage of LinkedIn to promote your brand and yourself? How should you integrate your other social networks, your website, and your blog as well as your off-site marketing with LinkedIn?

In the past people used Rolodex cards, Excel spreadsheets, boxes of business cards, and dozens of other things to maintain their business contacts. Networking was done in person or over the phone, and job-hunting consisted of the agonizing routine of mailing out thousands of resumes and hoping someone responded.

I attended hundreds of networking events and courses, spending much of my time collecting bags full of business cards, always intending to contact these people later and add them to my network. Almost invariably, the cards got shoved into a drawer, and other priorities took over until they finally got shoveled into the trash can.

Of course, people still do all those things, but now there is a better way to brand yourself to make others aware of who you are, what you're selling and what services you offer.

You may have a blog, or possibly a website, and you might even have Facebook and Twitter accounts as well as other social networks. However, I'll bet you haven't tied them together in a way that supports your brand, as well as the sales of your products and services.

Use LinkedIn to define your personal brand and explain it in short, simple terms so that people become intrigued with you, want to find out more, and want to connect. Business relationships result from these connections, and this can lead to purchases of your products and services, locating new employees and consultants, and finding new vendors.

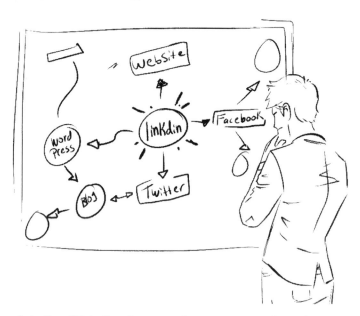

You can think of LinkedIn as the center of a wheel, and each of the other social networks is a spoke of that wheel. Other networks such as Facebook, Google+,

Twitter, and so on should reference your LinkedIn profile. The idea is to drive as much traffic as possible to LinkedIn.

Your LinkedIn profile should reference your blog and website, on which you presumably sell your products and services. The result is that traffic flows from your other social networks to LinkedIn and then to your site or blog.

By tying together all of your social networks, your website (or multiple websites), your blog, and everything else that defines you and your brand online, you can create a consistent view describing precisely the information that you want other people to know and understand. Each social network has a different audience and is made up of another type of social interaction, and you can take advantage of each as you see fit.

Also, by skillfully positioning links you can favor one network over another. Thus, if you wanted to drive people to your LinkedIn page, you could place the URL near the top of your web page in an extremely visible location. By positioning links to your other social networking sites lower down on the page, perhaps in the footer, you deemphasize them to your readers. You then have the option of moving links up or down on pages in your website depending on your needs.

If you've written your LinkedIn profile correctly, using the appropriate keywords and key phrases, you'll find that it will, in time, appear very high in search engine listings. For example, as of this writing, searching on Google (or Bing or another search engine) using my name, brings up my LinkedIn profile as the first entry in the search results, with my blogs, websites, and social media accounts appearing lower down.

This characteristic is one of the reasons why it is imperative that you spend the time to make sure your LinkedIn profile is well-written. People who look for you in search engines will find your LinkedIn profile near the top of the listing, making it more likely they will visit that site to get information about you.

Strategy

LinkedIn is just one component of a strategy to help you achieve your business and professional goals. Although it's a critical piece of the puzzle of branding yourself, take the time to form a coherent strategy to extend your reach even further.

Begin your plan by defining your target audience and your message (brand) and work from there. If the people you're trying to reach are C-level executives, then your strategy may be quite different than if you are attempting to get people to purchase your books or services. The features and tools provided by LinkedIn may be enough for one audience while another might require a blog and regular posting to other social media sites.

Make the decision whether or not you want to maintain a blog, but be wary, as they can be a lot of work. To create a blog you need to find a web host (I would not recommend the hosted version of WordPress at wordpress.com), choose a platform such as WordPress or Drupal, hire an expert or learn how to use it, and maintain the site. All of this is all in addition to writing blog articles; as you can see a blog can be a lot of work.

Maintaining a website is even more labor-intensive, requiring specialized knowledge of tools, programming languages, and techniques.

One way to get around updating a blog or maintaining a website is to write articles on LinkedIn using the post functionality. By doing this, you're effectively writing your blog on LinkedIn itself.

There are also social media platforms such as Facebook, Google+ and hundreds, if not thousands, of others. Each one of these requires effort to maintain and keep up-to-date. Different markets need various social media platforms; for example, Goodreads is critical for a writer to sell books while technical forums are important for engineers and programmers.

Don't forget about keeping your resume and business cards up-to-date, and if you are marketing products or services, you'll need to have a current media packet or catalog ready to send to customers.

Everything you do requires work and time, and possibly money. It is better to focus on just a few effective channels rather than try and deal with them all. For my writing services, for example, LinkedIn, Goodreads, and a blog are the best combinations. Other industries will have different needs.

It is important as you move forward in time to keep good records, so you know what is working and what is not producing results.

None of this is a one-time activity. It is important to keep your LinkedIn, targeted social media, and your blog (as well as your resume) up-to-date at all times. You never know when somebody's going to run across that profile or because they need precisely the skills that you provide. It's best to be ready for those instances at a moment's notice.

If you understand your audience, and more importantly you know who they are, then your message and your brand communicate naturally to those people or groups. On the other hand, if you don't know who you're talking to, or you don't have a clear message, then don't be surprised if your efforts to market your products services or yourself don't go very far.

People have written whole volumes about marketing strategy on both a personal, professional and business level. The information, tools, and techniques are two varied to go into in this volume but suffice to say that you'll need to have at least a simple strategy to leverage your brand to meet your goal.

Allowing Others to See You

Being noticed is the purpose of creating a profile on LinkedIn because that can lead to connections, which leads to conversations and communication, which can lead to job offers, selling products or services, hiring consultants, or any number of other desirable outcomes.

LinkedIn will show you who has viewed your profile recently, and under most conditions, it's wise to allow others to see that you have seen theirs.

In the privacy and settings section of LinkedIn, you can set whether you want to remain anonymous or let others know that you have viewed their online profile.

Use the following link for instructions on how to change this setting:

https://goo.gl/EEPQXx

There are reasons to remain anonymous.
Recruiters might not want employees of a company to know that they were looking at their profiles for possible recruitment purposes, or a human resources employee might check out a profile to make sure that it didn't violate any company policies.

Writing up Your Brand

"The keys to brand success are self-definition, transparency, authenticity and accountability." — **Simon Mainwaring, Author, We First**

Sometimes I am appalled by the profiles that I see on LinkedIn. Many consist only of a list of employers with a few dates and possibly a short sentence or two. The worst offenders are completely blank except for a name, and others contain fluff or sales-oriented materials.

I understand that it can be difficult to write your personal brand – schools don't teach this talent. In fact, our society often frowns on people who talk about themselves in glowing terms, and unless you're famous, it is socially unacceptable to "toot your own horn."

Nonetheless, the purpose of LinkedIn is to tell people about your strengths, skills, and how you can be of service to others. It's imperative that you tell others about yourself and accurately state your abilities in positive terms.

What is the best way to do this on LinkedIn? Let's begin with some of the things you shouldn't do.

LinkedIn is not a sales tool. There is no capability to include a storefront, to list products, or to add a shopping cart or checkout. If you're thinking of LinkedIn as a method to help you sell, then you're going to be sorely disappointed.

Additionally, LinkedIn is not intended to reproduce your resume. I know this seems counterintuitive since one of the purposes of the website is to help you find employment or to help employers find prospects. But the site is not designed for resumes; the idea is to supplement your job search, not reproduce other job hunting sites.

Okay, if it's not for resumes and sales, how do you use it effectively? LinkedIn is a marketing tool used to define the personal brand of individuals. You can think of it as a personal brand social media site.

What does this mean? LinkedIn is about you and is intended to showcase your unique skills, abilities and experience in the best possible light so that others become interested in networking with you professionally.

Keep this in mind while you work on your profile and as you keep it current day after day, week after week and over the years. LinkedIn is not Facebook – the two social networks perform very different functions.

Keywords and phrases

As you design and write your LinkedIn profile, think about words and phrases that people will type into search engines to find out about you. These are called keywords and phrases. Make an effort to sprinkle them throughout your profile – in the headline, position titles, summary, experiences, and each of the other sections.

Do not attempt to "fool" the search engines by listing keywords or stuffing as many as you can into the text. Search engines caught onto spamming of this nature a long time ago, and it could cause your page to be dropped down in the rankings.

In the text, use the words and phrases naturally as part of your writing, and use them in your headline and the titles (with each experience.)

One trick to coming up with good keywords is to get your current job description (or search the web) and use a tool called *Wordle* to give you the most important words and phrases. *Google Keyword Planner* (part of AdWords) is also an excellent, albeit somewhat complicated, keyword tool.

Personal Details

I've already said this, but I will state it again because it's important. It's a good idea to refrain from including more than a few selected personal details in your LinkedIn profile. While part of branding yourself is showing that you are a human being – a few personal details can serve that purpose – take care not to go overboard. In this case, a small amount goes a long way.

The Headline

Your headline is one of the first things displayed by search engines. It's vital that this small, 120 character, description be accurate, robust, and descriptive of your brand. LinkedIn, Google, and other search engines show the headline as part of their search results; this may be the first, and the only thing that people see and they will use it to judge whether or not to review the rest of your profile.

Essentially, your headline needs to summarize what you offer to others into those 120 characters. Many people waste this valuable space by including just their job title or function; it's better to include a list of the most important aspects of your brand in addition to your title.

Include your job title in your headline if it's descriptive of your personal brand or the image that you're trying to portray. However, if the title is not representative of your brand, then you can either shorten it or eliminate it entirely.

You can get more space for keywords and phrases by abbreviating certain terms. For example, shorten

"Vice President" to VP, "Executive" to "Exec." and "Administrator" to "Admin."

Avoid words fluff words such as motivated, responsible, track record, driven, expert and so on. These don't communicate anything of value, and their meanings are not clear. Use focused keywords and phrases to get the point across more precisely.

A good headline describes what you do and provides viewers with an instant understanding of your strengths. Think about keywords, which are words and phrases that others use when they search for people with your skills, abilities, and experiences. Some good key phrases are "Senior SQL Engineer", or "MCSA Certified Systems Administrator", or "Senior Ghostwriter." The idea is to use words and phrases which can be used to find you on the Internet and within LinkedIn.

Separate keywords or phrases with a delimiter. Some people use a star or an asterisk while others use graphics characters in another font. Separating phrases in this way makes them stand out and thereby looks impressive. Be sure to leave a space on either side of the delimiter so your headline doesn't appear crowded.

My headline is:

CEO, Senior Writer ✔ *Ghostwriter* ✓ *Speaker* ✓ *LinkedIn Branding Expert* ✓ *Blogger* ✓ *Computer Security* ► *LION*

By looking at this, you can tell which skills and abilities I possess. You immediately know that I'm a senior writer, author, ghostwriter, speaker and a LinkedIn Branding expert as well as a blogger and know how to make a computer secure. The word LION stands for LinkedIn Open Networker. It means that I accept connection requests from people I don't know.

Most headlines will be far simpler since it is a usually best to focus your LinkedIn profile narrowly.

Another example:

Senior SQL DBA ✓ Performance ✓ ETL & Cube Processing ✓ Cloud Computing ✓ Experienced Database Administrator

Sprinkle your keywords and phrases throughout the remainder of your LinkedIn profile. Include them in your summary, experiences, projects, and anywhere else they make sense. Don't just list them; write them naturally into each section, such that everything flows well. Your target audience is both human beings and automated robots; you must make each part understandable to people as well as to robots such as the Google search engine. By including keywords and phrases, you give these robots (or spiders) the information they need to index your profile.

Do not become stressed about what to include in your headline. It's simple to change, and you should feel free to do so if it's not proving to be effective in getting you leads, job offers or customers.

Instructions for changing your LinkedIn headline are at the following link:

https://goo.gl/8X8VRN

Your Photo

You know what they say, first impressions are the most important, and LinkedIn is no exception. In fact, the rapid pace of the Internet and new technology makes it vital that the first glance creates a positive view. You may have less than two or three seconds for someone to decide whether to click or move on. Their decision will be based almost entirely on your headline and your photo.

Some of the profile pictures that I see on LinkedIn, as well as on other sites, cause me to shake my head in bewilderment. Finding a job, getting a sale or making an important connection can depend upon the quality of your photograph. Take the time, and perhaps spend a little money, to get it right.

Don't use a picture in which other people are visible or have been cropped out.

Don't use pictures with your office, computer screen, a bar, restaurant, or other cluttered locations in the background.

Don't use selfies. These look amateur because the lighting is poor, your arms may be in strange positions, and you may look contorted.

Unprofessional photographs tend to have poor lighting, strangely placed shadows, poorly posed positions, cluttered backgrounds, and strange facial expressions.

If you can afford it, hire a professional photographer who takes headshots or portraits for a living. Find a good one, and look at samples of their work.

The area to the rear of your head and body is just as important as your image. What kind of impression do you think a messy house, a bar, a blank brick wall with graffiti, or even a cemetery gives to a viewer?

The background should be plain or abstract, with nothing identifiable other than a plain or colored pattern. A professional photographer will know how to bring out the best based on your skin color, hair color and so forth. The idea is to make sure there's nothing behind you that overpowers your image or that gives people an incorrect impression of your brand and you.

Your pose in the photo depends on your brand. A circus clown will have a far different look than the CEO of a multi-billion dollar company. An actor or actress might appear dramatic; a model might be staring off into the distance while a professional business person would sit comfortably.

The clothing that you wear for the shoot also depends on your brand. Engineers might dress casually; a business person in professional attire, whereas a dancer might be wearing his or her dance outfit.

If you can't hire a professional, then get someone else to take the photo – selfies are never appropriate – and don't rush it. Find a good background, and ensure that you take several hundred pictures. After all, cameras these days are digital, and there is no additional cost for the extra photos. Once you have the images, look through them and find the one that is perfect for your brand.

If you take your photos outdoors, pose in the shade out of direct sunlight. Harsh lighting will make you look older in your picture.

Watch out for the effects of the camera flash, which include redeye and hotspots (unnaturally white areas, often on the face.) Also, be careful of shadows that can make you look older or tired.

Unless you're going for a particular look for your brand, ensure that you look happy. Avoid looking tired, depressed, upset and don't glare or scowl at the camera. Sometimes you will think you are smiling, but that smile won't show well in the finished photo. That's another reason it's a good idea to use a second person to take the picture – they can verify your facial expressions and smile.

Finally, it's best to look to one side or the other of the camera, but not at the ceiling or floor. Looking directly at the camera can be unnerving to the viewer, and looking down can be taken as a sign of weakness or disinterest.

Most important of all, don't rush and don't be afraid to eliminate photos that do not show you at your best. If that means you have to throw them all away and do it again, well, shoot some more photos. After all, digital photos do not need to be developed and don't cost any money.

Use tools such as Photoshop and other image editors to touch up blemishes, cleanup shadows, and improve a photo. Don't go overboard and make it look unnatural or obviously photoshopped. But a few quick touchups can vastly improve even a great picture.

Go to the link below for information on how to add or change your profile photo:

https://goo.gl/1Fn82k

Summarizing your Brand

The purpose of your summary is not to impress your peers or subordinates. The goal is to gain the interest of potential employers or customers.

You must understand the nature of your audience. Before you write one word of your summary, visualize the people who will be reading what you have written. Who is going to hire you, purchase your product or services, or in some other way engage in business with you? Those people are your audience. Keep that picture in mind as you plan and write your summary.

One of the most common mistakes when writing the summary is to pull a couple of paragraphs from your resume and paste them directly into the summary, perhaps with a few words changed here and there. Resumes are stiffly formal, written in the third person, and contain far too much information for LinkedIn.

Don't just write a few sentences or paragraphs without putting much thought into it. Spend the time and write a summary which truly communicates the benefit you provide to others and your unique skills and abilities.

If you are not going to take the time to do it right, then leave your summary blank. Making no impression is better than making a poor impression. Just remember to come back later and update it, because a professionally written summary is very powerful for branding, finding business and gaining leads.

Most of the time you spend working on your LinkedIn profile should be spent writing, revising and proofreading your summary. This section is displayed at the "top of the fold", which means it is the first thing shown on the screen. Sometimes the summary, the headline, and the photo are the only things that a viewer will see.

Write you're summary in the first person because you're telling people about yourself and your personal brand. By speaking to your reader as if you were in a conversation with them, you put them at ease, and thus they become more receptive to what you have to say.

There are many different philosophies as to how to write an excellent summary on LinkedIn. There is no right and wrong, no black and white and no magic prescription for how to write one.

Start with a boldly written paragraph that describes your industry or profession, why it's important and where it's going. Someone in the retail industry, for example, might write that technology is changing the way shoppers find and purchase products while another person in the medical field might mention the competition between hospitals and how new legislation by the government has changed the delivery, price and service level of hospital care.

By doing this, you establish yourself as keeping your eye on the ball with an understanding of the future of your industry. It generates a certain aura of respect and adds credence to your knowledge and responsibility.

Next, introduce yourself and summarize your credentials by briefly stating your experience, unique skills and so forth. Give your reader the understanding that you are the person who can solve their problem or meet their needs.

Include statistics that demonstrate results. If possible, include numbers that prove your success. Think about successful clients, money earned, improved profit margins, and reduced headcounts. Statistics such as these are extremely powerful and prove you get results.

Now spend a little bit of time reinforcing what you've already written by including a few major accomplishments throughout your career. The purpose of this is to add credibility to support what you've already stated.

Wrap it all up by summarizing in a sentence or two how you stand out from your competition, why you would be a good fit, and how you can help potential employers or prospects.

End your summary with a call to action. You want your reader to do something: tell them to give you a call, send you an email, connect with you on LinkedIn or whatever. You need to tell them what you want them to do. At a minimum, tell them to send you an email (and include your email address.)

Your call to action can be as simple as:

Please connect with me on LinkedIn today or send an email to rich@richardlowe.com

It's a good idea to avoid specialized technical language, or, at least, keep it to a minimum. Remember, even if you're an extremely skilled engineer, the people who want to hire you may be managers or customers who do not possess your knowledge. You are not trying to impress other engineers; you're attempting to get the attention of the people who are going to hire you, purchase your services, or buy your products.

Quantifying your Experience

In the experience sections, it is very common for people to copy text from their resume into the profile. While it might seem expedient, it is counterproductive and doesn't make the best advantage of the power of LinkedIn.

Reinforce goal and message you defined while planning your branding strategy. Everything you write in your profile should reinforce this objective in one way or another.

Enhance and support what you've stated in your summary. Use the space in each experience to tell a story about how that position supports your personal brand. Focus most of your attention on those jobs that illustrate your background, skills, and achievements as they pertain to your overall goal and message.

If a position that doesn't support or enhance your brand, then don't spend a lot of time discussing it in your experiences section. Include the experience because it's best to avoid gaps in your employment record, but don't go into great detail about it - unless you can somehow show how it helped with your growth or abilities.

The exception is your current or most recent position; always thoroughly write this up as it describes what you are doing now, and it is the first job your readers will see after viewing the summary (assuming you put your summary on top of your profile.)

You can document how a position that you've held – even if it has nothing to do with what you're trying to achieve – adds credibility to your brand. For example, I began my career in the computer industry, was eventually promoted to Vice President of the company, and then spent twenty years working at Trader Joe's. I left that position to become a writer, which is a significant change in careers. I illustrate throughout my LinkedIn profile, especially in the experiences section, how the positions in my past helped prepare me to be a better writer by giving me experience in management, technical areas, and dealing with people.

Be sure that your profile doesn't get in the way of finding a position or customers; unfortunately, too much information may cause you to be excluded rather than included. Some managers semi-jokingly refer to his as being over qualified.

If you are currently unemployed – or for those annoying gaps in employment – create an entry to fill in the time. You might write that you were a consultant or freelancer, or even establish a company of your own and write a description of it. Doing this is much better than leaving holes in your job experience. Just ensure that whatever your write is truthful.

 Visit the following link for instructions on how to edit your experience:

https://goo.gl/g2oTfJ

Adding a Background Image

Did you know you can add a background image to your LinkedIn profile? Adding an image can be used to reinforce your branding or to add a little color or pizzazz to your profile.

The information on the LinkedIn profile covers most of the image, except for a thin strip just over the top and a small bit on each side. That's not much room, but it still can be used effectively. Keep in mind that on different platforms, different browsers, and different zoom factors more or less of the image may appear. In fact, under some conditions, the image may not show at all.

One option is to find a picture on a free stock photo site such as pixabay.com and use that as your background image. By adding a simple pattern with some color, you make your profile stand out a little bit.

Another

You can use a background which represents your business or brand. The following graphic would be descriptive for a warehousing company, for example.

You can create a picture to make your brand pop out of the page. To help promote that I'm an author, I made an image with the cover of one of my books on the left side and a few words describing my brand on the right. It's short, simple and reinforces my brand.

Feel free to get creative by adding an image of your book cover, a graph, a chart or some other graphic that illustrates your products, services or skills. There's not a lot of room, and the quality is not exceptionally high, but it is useful to reinforce your message.

See the following page for instructions on how to add your background image:

https://goo.gl/ooaZZf

Your Education, Certifications, and Courses

Education

Over the course of the thirty-five years of my career in the IT industry, I hired several hundred people and examined tens of thousands of resumes. The sections on education were often an enigma and usually were not very useful.

People spend a significant part of their lives, four to ten years, earning a degree in one or more colleges or universities. However, on the resume that vast amount of time and potentially hundreds of classes was boiled down to just a few lines which name schools, degrees, and majors.

The resume – or LinkedIn profile – might show that a person went to a prestigious school, earned a degree, and received a Ph.D. However, normally there were no details on the quality of the education, the courses attended, or even the subject of the Ph.D. thesis. For example, my boss, who was the VP of Information Technology, earned a music degree in college, and his resume stated he had a Bachelor's degree. This degree had little or nothing to do with his current role, yet it was impossible to discern this fact from what he had written.

Always include your colleges, even if you didn't graduate, on your LinkedIn profile. Anything before college is usually not crucial or pertinent unless you are just starting out in the professional world. I wouldn't recommend including anything from high school or before except under special circumstances.

As with your experiences section, write a story for each school you attended which reinforces your branding message. Keep it short and simple, and directed towards your overall goal.

Mention activities, classes, and assignments which are pertinent to your brand. For example, if you are a Senior Engineer, and your thesis was on something related to engineering, document it in the description for the school (or add it in the publication's section.) Doing this will add to your credibility in the area of your expertise.

On the other hand, things which are not pertinent to your personal brand should be mentioned sparingly, if at all.

Use your judgment about what facts to include in your education. Just keep in mind that quite too much information can be used to exclude candidates rather than include.

 Visit the following link for instructions on how to modify your education:

https://goo.gl/enUSpC

Certifications

Always list any certifications that you've earned, especially if they pertain directly to your personal brand. If you are a project manager, for example, include that you have received the PMP (Project Management Professional) certification. Similarly, if you are in a field that relies on certifications, such as a CPA or specialist in computers, then definitely show any of them that you have earned.

Throughout my career, there has been an ongoing *debate* as to the value of getting certified. When I look at a resume, one of the features that cause prospects to stand out from the crowd is the list of their certifications. Not only does this add validation to their skills and knowledge, but it also speaks highly of their motivation for keeping up-to-date in their industry. A steady progression of certifications earned over many years, updated regularly, provided valuable insight into how engaged a person has been throughout their career.

Let's take a computer professional, for example. An absence of certifications can be a red flag in a hiring situation. The world of computers is changing rapidly, and constant updates of knowledge are essential. A dearth of classes and certifications means the professional is not bothering to keep their skills up-to-date. In my opinion, this lowers their employability.

Certifications that are long out-of-date are another red flag, indicating a lack of engagement in furthering their career. Several years ago, I received a resume from a gentleman who'd been a system administrator for twenty years. His certifications were for an ancient and obsolete version of the operating system, obtained from his first job, but he had not attended any classes since that time. I passed him over and hired a different applicant who kept his certifications up-to-date.

The ideal situation is to have certifications in the relevant industry, and perhaps some related areas, which are up-to-date to the newest versions of the technology in the field.

I was interviewing a person for an IT position involving the Oracle database. He had certifications for both the SQL and Oracle databases, as well as Windows system administration. During the interview, he mentioned that he found understanding the operating system allowed him to do a better job of administering the database. Because of this extra knowledge, he was aware of some of the externally enforced limitations on what he could do as a DBA. Thus, the Windows certifications added credibility to his experience and knowledge, even though they were not essential to his career.

 Review this page for instructions about certifications:

https://goo.gl/UK26iP

Courses

In LinkedIn, you can include a list of courses that you've attended. You can associate these with any position in your experience section and any education you've received. You can also choose not to associate them with anything.

As with everything on LinkedIn regarding your personal brand, be careful not to go too far and list every single course that you've ever taken. Boil down your courses to those things that reinforce your brand, possibly including a few others to show that you have interests elsewhere.

Include any continuing education courses you have taken to support your career. As with certifications, keeping up-to-date with your knowledge shows that you are interested in your career, the companies you work for, and your industry. It shows you are engaged, active, and willing to spend the time needed to remain up-to-date and current.

Your URL

By default, LinkedIn assigns a URL (web address) of your name combined with a few numbers to make it unique. Change this URL to something more pertinent and meaningful.

Ideally, use your first and last name. If taken, try your first, middle initial and last name, or your first name, middle name and last name. If worst comes to worst, you can tack on another word such as "writer" or "architect". I recommend against using numbers or random strings of characters because it's difficult to remember.

Don't use dots or dashes because people will often forget to include them, and this may cause them to bring up to the wrong LinkedIn profile.

Since LinkedIn is for personal branding, avoid using your company or some cute saying or phrase. It's best to stick to your name for LinkedIn.

Use this URL for your promotional materials both on the web and off-line, including your business cards, brochures, flyers and anything else you use for marketing purposes.

For example, my URL on LinkedIn is as follows:

https://www.linkedin.com/in/richardlowejr

Which is much better than:

https://www.linkedin.com/in/richard.lowe-9273974389

 Visit the link below for instructions on changing your URL:

https://goo.gl/C8kGPz

Contact Information

There are two areas for you to use to showcase your contact information: the Contact Info section into which you can enter your basic information; and the Advice for Contacting, which is freeform text to give you plenty of room to detail how to get hold of you. Also, it's a good idea to include your email address at the end of your summary section in a call to action.

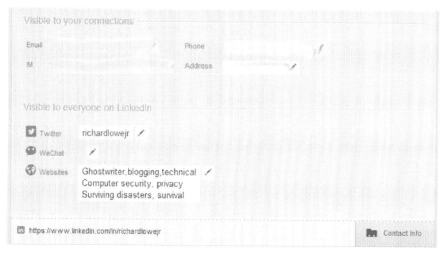

Fill in as much of your contact information as necessary in the contact info area, because that is the first place people will look when they want to get hold of you.

Include the advice for contacting, even if the information is redundant, to give additional details. There's plenty of room in both places to provide details including phone numbers, your fax number, website addresses, messaging services such as Skype and email address.

Advice for Contacting Richard

Feel free to send a connection request even if we have not met.

I am a professional writer and a ghostwriter. If you need technical writing, a book ghostwritten, articles for your blog, and so on, please connect with me on LinkedIn.

Email: rich@thewritingking.com
Phone: (727) 475-6487 • FAX: (727) 324 6629
Email: inquiry@thewritingking.com
Skype: richardlowejrwriter

Web Sites:
✓ Professional website: https://www.thewritingking.com/
✓ Personal Blog: https://www.richardlowe.com/
✓ Security Blog: http://www.leavemycomputeralone.com/
✓ Survival Blog: https://www.realworldsurvival.com/
✓ Published works: http://www.coolauthor.com/

Don't overdo it by adding more than one or two email address or phone numbers. Just include your primary contact methods.

I'm amazed at the number of people who don't fill out these sections, which can make it difficult to communicate with them outside of LinkedIn.

LinkedIn supports InMail for messaging, but if the receiver is outside of your network and not in one of your groups, there's a charge associated with sending a message.

It's quite common for people not to receive or respond to messages from LinkedIn for days, weeks or even months. Many people adjust the LinkedIn settings to avoid receiving email notifications (there can be quite a lot of them in an active account), and some never check their LinkedIn inbox at all.

Solve this problem by ensuring you list your other contact information. You can include your email, phone number, Skype address or other instant messaging handle.

List up to three websites in the contact area in your profile. For SEO purposes, choose the "other" option from the drop-down and type in keywords for each site. Search engines such as Google consider this to be anchor text, which gives your websites a slight boost on your keywords.

Be cautious about including personal phone numbers or home addresses on your LinkedIn profile. A home address should never be used publicly on LinkedIn, as it's unwise to give out that information to strangers. Scammers and other nefarious individuals look through social media regularly to find personal information, and if they find a home address they may target you and your loved ones for various crimes.

 See this page for instructions on changing your contact information:

https://goo.gl/Ax2CgP

A note on email addresses

Your email address is part of your personal branding. An AOL, HOTMAIL or a similar address is considered amateur. Many people use GMAIL addresses, which is at least more modern.

The best strategy is to use a unique domain name chosen specifically for your brand. Domain names are not expensive, and if you purchase web hosting, you'll usually get a domain thrown as a "freebie."

For example, I use two different domains names: one for my company, richard@thewritingking.com, *and the other,* rich@richardlowe.com, *for personal use.*

If you do use a personal email address, ensure it is professional, even if you need to create a new one. Do not include sexual innuendos, jokes, profanity, movie titles or characters as part of the name and avoid numbers, dots and dashes if possible.

Projects

Another way to document your expertise, which reinforces your brand, is to include projects that you've completed throughout your education and career. These give you added credibility, strengthen your skills and experience, and give you extra room to expand upon aspects of your career.

Projects display in a list underneath each experience or educational section in your profile. A viewer has to click a button to see them, so they are often ignored. However, if someone is interested and wants more details, they can click a link to get them.

As a general rule, it's best to keep the description of your project short and to the point. You don't need a lot of text to fulfill the goal of adding credibility to your profile and brand. A paragraph or two, at the most, is more than adequate.

As with everything else, make sure the projects that you include are adding value to the message and brand that you are trying to communicate. Too many projects tend to clutter up the profile with extraneous or redundant information, and a large variety of unrelated projects can make you look scattered and unfocused.

 Read the following page for instructions about editing projects.

https://goo.gl/ukFuyc

Skills and Endorsements

The Skills and Endorsements section of your profile is intended to be a list of keywords and phrases highlighting your skills and abilities. You can list up to fifty of them, and they can be in any order that you like.

LinkedIn shows the first ten at the top of your list when it displays them to visitors. The assumption is the top ten are the most important skills, and LinkedIn makes them stand out for easy recognition.

As you use LinkedIn, you'll notice that you are occasionally prompted to endorse the skills of some of your connections. It's pretty simple to click the okay button to add your endorsement to their skills.

The idea of Skills and Endorsements is to demonstrate that others have agreed you perform those skills. The greater the number next to each skill, the more people have endorsed you.

I don't spend a lot of time worrying about skills. In my profile, I added the ones that made sense, ordered them into the correct sequence, and then forgot about them. I'm certain skills don't hurt, and they may even help a bit, but since people tend to click the okay button blindly when asked to endorse, in my opinion their value is not very high.

Always include this section in your profile and spend a little bit of time ensuring the list makes sense and is in the correct order. But I wouldn't recommend spending time trying to get people to endorse them. I prefer to depend on LinkedIn's automatic endorsement features.

 Read the following link for instructions on adding and removing skills:

https://goo.gl/INa9Tj

All the Other Entries

There are many other entries that you can include in your LinkedIn profile. Each of these can be used to reinforce your personal brand and add evidence to support what you've written about yourself.

Honors and awards

If you have received any honors and awards, include them in your profile. You have room to write quite a bit of information if you want, but it is usually best to keep it short. Spend some time writing a brief explanation in the form of a story to demonstrate the value of that honor award.

Take care not to overdo it. If you have received more than a few awards, more than half a dozen, pick the most prestigious or significant ones and include those on your profile.

Listing a few honors and awards adds credibility to your personal brand and backs up your claims for your expertise and skills.

Make a point of contributing to your business, charities and groups and, in the process, gain a few honors and awards. These are useful not just in your LinkedIn profile but for improving your self-confidence and abilities.

Patents

Include any patents awarded to you in the patent section of LinkedIn, especially if they add to your personal brand. For example, if you're an engineer with a patent on a new type of application for smartphones, then include the details here.

Don't go overboard on adding patents. In this section shorter is better. One or two of these which directly relate to the story you've created about yourself will go a long way, but more than that will make your profile seem cluttered and overbearing.

Organizations

This section allows you to show the organizations you support. By being involved, and by including it in your LinkedIn profile, you confirm that you are a team member and can work with others.

As with other sections, don't go overboard and list dozens of organizations just because you signed up for their mailing list or visited their office a few times. Include those that add credibility to your brand or that show you have interests in the community, the nation, your church, or business in general.

Not listing any organizations at all can be slightly detrimental in that it shows that you're not taking an interest in anything outside of the narrow focus of your job. By joining and being active in organizations, you contribute to others, and this makes you a more well-rounded individual.

Publications

Include any publications that you've written or that others have written about you in this section. Include podcasts, self-published books, papers, white papers, interviews, articles, videos, or anything else that applies to your brand.

Don't go overboard – a few significant listings go a long way. Too many items will make your profile appear crowded and overbearing.

Keep this list focused on things that reinforce your personal brand, although a few publications that are unrelated demonstrates you have interests outside of your job or business.

You can consolidate several articles or interviews into a single listing to cause your profile to look a little less overbearing. By doing this, you can demonstrate that you have been featured many times without cluttering up your profile.

Volunteer

Well-rounded individuals tend to volunteer for various organizations because they believe in the cause or want to help. While it doesn't hurt to leave this section blank, if you're a person who likes to volunteer then it is helpful to list those organizations here.

Languages

Listing any languages that you speak, or can read or write, opens up additional possibilities for employment or, if you sell services, may widen your market. Include them in this section, and be honest about your proficiency with the language. Don't overstate how well you speak, read or write because you may be asked to use those skills later.

What is the Best Order?

LinkedIn allows you to put the various sections of your profile in any order that you want. Since most people read from the top down to the bottom, you'll want to organize it so that the most important things are near the top and the least important or at the bottom. In other words, arrange the sections in descending order of importance.

The photo, headline, your name, positions, education, contact info and a list of the post that you created always appear at the top of your profile. You cannot change the order of these sections.

At the bottom, LinkedIn always shows recommendations, connections, groups and who you are following. The sections are also in the same order for everyone.

The summary is by far the most significant block of information in your profile, and you should always place it as close to the top as possible. Your summary is the statement defining your personal brand to your audience and thus is the first thing that you want people to read.

For most people, their experience is more important than the education they received, especially if the schooling occurred more than a few years (or a few jobs) in the past. In general, this means your experience should be placed immediately following the summary, Honors and Awards, and Projects should be next in line.

Languages may or may not be critical to your career path. If being multilingual is relevant to your position, then move the languages section up higher. Otherwise, place it just below the experience related blocks.

Your organizations and volunteering activities should probably come next in most cases. If your brand centers around volunteering and nonprofit work, you may want to move these blocks higher.

Your educational history belongs relatively close to the bottom of your profile. Obviously, schooling is important but in virtually all cases experience trumps education. Certifications and courses should be positioned ahead of the Education section since they contain more current information as a rule.

The very last blocks in your profile should be the additional information sections as well as the advice for contacting block. If someone reads through your entire profile gets to the bottom, you want to give them your contact information because they are probably very interested in what you have to say.

Remember that you can move each of the sections around anytime you want. So if you later determine that one block should be placed higher for whatever reason, you can just go ahead and move it up or move something else down.

Just make sure that the elements that are relevant to your brand are higher up in the profile and those that have lesser importance are lower down.

It's About Relationships

"One of the challenges in networking is everybody thinks it's making cold calls to strangers. Actually, it's the people who already have strong trust relationships with you, who know you're dedicated, smart, a team player, who can help you." — **Reid Hoffman, Author, The Start-up of You: Adapt to the Future, Invest in Yourself, and Transform Your Career**

The purpose of LinkedIn is to build and maintain relationships, specifically those that are professional and business-oriented. It's useful to compare the way you would interact socially in the real world with the virtual world of LinkedIn.

Consider for a moment that you are attending a business social event. Would you want to look your best so that people have a good impression? Or would you wear torn up clothes and dirty shoes? Would you have showered recently? And would you have plenty of your business cards available to hand out?

Think of your LinkedIn profile in the same way. You want to make sure that you have your summary polished and describing you and your brand precisely. Your experiences should be complete and descriptive and, if possible, reinforce your message about you and your roles at other companies.

There are two ways that you will gain relationships on LinkedIn. People will send you a connection request because they find your profile, and you will send others connection requests because you find them of interest for some reason.

Building and maintaining your network on LinkedIn is a never ending task, which is essentially the same as in the real world. To keep your connections fresh and useful, you have to put an effort on a regular basis.

Plan on spending anywhere from thirty minutes to several hours a week updating information into LinkedIn. Make changes to your profile, add a status update occasionally, write a post once in a while, and add and comment on discussions and groups. These activities will cause your connections to engage with you, which could lead to business opportunities.

Contact Information

To allow people to communicate with you make sure your contact information is up-to-date. The contact details area of LinkedIn is the equivalent of your business card, letting everyone know how they can get hold of you outside of LinkedIn.

All of the other information on your profile serves the purpose in letting people know who you are, what you represent, and what image you are portraying. By including accurate and interesting information, you entice others into connecting with you or contacting you by other means.

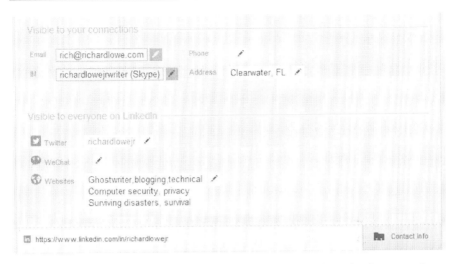

Refrain from posting personal connection information on LinkedIn (and on any other social network as well.) I recommend against including your home phone number, address, and if there's a choice, your personal email address. Doing so allows you to keep your work life and your personal life separate.

For example, it's not appropriate for patients to be calling their doctor via his cell phone in the middle of the evening or while he's on vacation. Including personal contact information on the doctor's profile gives his patients that option. Instead, include the phone number of the office or switchboard – when patients call the switchboard they are equipped to decide who is on-call and what to do.

Connection Requests

Think about connection requests and compare them to a social event. Would you shove your business cards in everyone's faces without an introduction? Would that be the best way to make connections with other people? Or do you think they would just crumple up your card and throw it away?

You can think of unsolicited connection requests without any explanation in the same way. These applications are likely to be ignored or not taken seriously. Oh sure, nine out of ten people will accept the connection, but since they don't know anything about you, the relationship is likely to be meaningless.

The right way to send an unsolicited connection request is to include a brief message describing who you are and why you want to connect. If you already know the person well, you won't need to say very much, but if you met once at a social event or exchanged business cards at a conference or class, it's a good idea to remind them by including a short note.

By explaining why you want to connect, or, at least, introducing yourself, you immediately start to build the online relationship. If you don't do this, then don't be surprised if the request is rejected, ignored or even reported as spam.

Once you have some connections, the next challenge is to build interest in what you have to say, and then to maintain their engagement. It's important to be constantly changing, adding and even removing information on LinkedIn, which will cause people to return to your profile on occasion, become reacquainted with you and your services, and make it more likely that they'll communicate further. They will ask questions, make comments, send you messages, and may even initiate a business relationship.

LinkedIn provides several ways to build and maintain engagement. The following sections describe some of these methods.

Notification of Updates and changes

Make changes to your profile regularly, even if you just add a few words, change your photo, or describe some of your projects. By doing this, you keep your profile fresh in the eyes of LinkedIn and search engines such as Google, and, depending on your settings, inform everyone in your network.

Search Engines

Google and other search engines scan all web pages regularly to see if anything has changed. As times goes by, web pages with changes tend to rank temporarily higher in search engine rankings, which means modified pages tend to show higher on the results pages of search engine than those that have not changed.

To ensure the people connected to you get notifications of changes, set "Notify Your Network..." to "YES." You will find that many of your followers will examine your profile to see what changed, make comments, and even send you a message.

A large number of changes in a short period can be a dead giveaway that you are searching for a job. In this case, you should turn off "Notify Your Network" by setting it to "NO" while making any significant changes. Turn it back to "ON" after you've finished. By doing this, you prevent notifications from being sent out to everyone while you are entering your updates.

Status updates

Posting brief status updates once or twice a week on business related topics is another good way to keep the engagement going. Many people use this to share links to articles that they find on the Internet. You can also let people know about any successes, classes, or things that you've learned.

Resist the impulse to post overly personal information. LinkedIn is for professional networking;

save your politics, math problems, and so forth for Facebook.

You can share your status updates with the entire public, just your connections, or with the entire public and your Twitter account.

Did you know you can mention other companies and users in your status updates? Just include the @ symbol immediately followed by the user or company name within your update. LinkedIn will send a notification to the user, and the status will include a link to their profile or page in the status update.

Posts

Another excellent feature is the ability to create a blog directly on LinkedIn. By posting short, non-promotional, business related articles on LinkedIn, you give the people in your network information that they may find to be of value. Sometimes this triggers a conversation about the services you provide or the potential for employment.

Posts

Published by Richard   1,121
See more ▸   followers

Writing a Book   **Enemies**   **Rejection is Part of a**
February 25, 2016   February 25, 2016   **Freelancers Life**
                                                  February 22, 2016

Choose subjects which are of interest to your followers in one way or another. Don't focus on selling; instead, provide information. The difference between marketing and sales is that marketing builds up your brand and reinforces your message while selling pushes your product. Never use LinkedIn for sales.

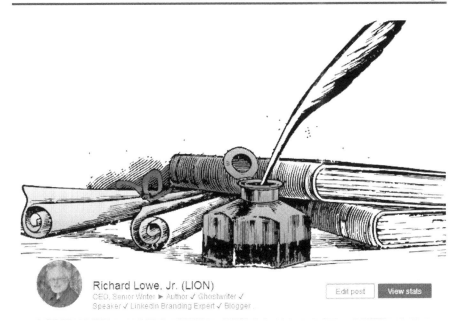

Richard Lowe, Jr. (LION)
CEO, Senior Writer ▶ Author ✓ Ghostwriter ✓
Speaker ✓ LinkedIn Branding Expert ✓ Blogger

Writing a Book

Feb 25, 2016 | 30 views   👍 2 Likes   💬 1 Comment

As of today, I have ghostwritten about a dozen books, written over 100 technical documents, and published 12 books of my own. I've got four books that are written and going through the review process and lots more planned.

Before writing your post, think about keywords and phrases, which can be useful in helping people to find your articles. Search engines use these keywords to build their index. For example, if your post is about job hunting, you might include three keywords: resumes, job hunting, and human resources.

As you write your post, use those keywords now and then. Don't just list them, use them as a natural part of your text.

Always include a photo or illustration for your post. Pixabay.com (and other similar sites) has millions of free public domain images. Make sure the image adds value to your text. For example, if the article is about anger management, an image of a shouting man would be perfect.

Look at the bottom of the post entry form to find a field allowing you to add as many as three tags. LinkedIn uses these to help categorize your article and distribute it to appropriate audiences. Always choose three categories. Feel free to change them as often as you like if you find they are not drawing traffic to your article.

You can add a signature to the bottom of your article which tells how to contact you, the name of your website, and the title and link to anything you've published. Keep the signature short and to the point, and try not to make it overly sales-oriented.

Sample Signature

Richard Lowe Jr is the CEO and Senior Writer for The Writing King, *and the author of* Safe Computing is Like Safe Sex *and* Real World Survival. *You can sign up for his* email newsletter, *which includes a weekly free podcast.*

Groups

Being active in *groups* is another great way to engage people both in and outside of your network. You can post questions or discussion topics in any group that you join, and you can comment on any discussion or question in those groups. You should do so on a regular basis as it will result in additional connections and engagement.

Some Notes About Updates and Posting

It is bad form to be overly promotional on LinkedIn. You wouldn't walk around a social event shoving flyers in the people's hands without at least striking up a conversation, would you? If you did so, you probably find that virtually all those pieces of paper wound up in the trash can.

Likewise, make sure any status updates, posts, discussions in groups, and other miscellaneous contributions lean more towards helping others, getting help from others, and providing some educational benefit.

Professionals enjoy helping others, so occasionally posting a question or request for some help of some sort helps build a rapport with your network.

It's also true that people enjoy receiving help, so answering a question now and then, or contributing in a positive manner to threads in groups, posts and updates will be appreciated.

You don't need to spend a lot of time performing these tasks. An hour or two a week, at the most, or even as little as thirty minutes, will fit the bill nicely. Rapidly scan over your groups, postings, and updates, and reply to anything where you can make a positive contribution.

Skip watching an hour or two of television each week, and spend that time updating your LinkedIn. It will have a far more positive impact on your profession and your life.

These tasks are relatively easy to outsource to a consultant, a virtual assistant, one of your staff, or company such as *LinkedIn Makeover*. Just provide good instructions, and, of course, check on it once a while to make sure it's what you need and want.

Your Blog, Website, and LinkedIn

"A key element of Web blogs is the community element. Most blogs are not self-contained; they are highly dependent on linking to each other." – **Evan Williams, Chairman and CEO of Twitter**

Most companies – and many individuals – maintain a blog or website, and sometimes both. These are essential for establishing a brand, selling products or services, and maintaining a relationship with customers, vendors, and others.

The contact area of LinkedIn allows for three links, which can include the address of your blog, your company website, or any other site on the web.

You can add additional links by putting them into the "advice for contacting..." area of your profile. You can also add links to any section, including the summary and experiences. However, LinknedIn only supports clickable hyperlinks in the three fields in the contact area.

Put your most important URLs in the three spots in your contact information. These will be clickable by visitors and indexed by search engines.

Authority

LinkedIn is considered an authority site by the major search engines such as Google. The websites associated with the URLs listed in the three positions in your contact area will gain slightly in ranking.

Blog or Website

A blog is a type of website regularly updated with articles and information, usually about a single topic. The most common blogging platform is WordPress, although there are dozens of others which serve the same purpose.

A website is typically more complex, often including a storefront, as well as information about the company and such.

These days it is becoming more common to create full-blown websites in platforms such as WordPress. That's because it's relatively straightforward to create a gorgeous and dynamic site using WordPress extensions (plugins, themes, and widgets.)

While you can create full-fledged websites using WordPress, it's better to create them using tools specifically for that purpose. They tend to be faster, friendlier to the user and have better support for backend databases.

Using Websites With LinkedIn

If you maintain a website separate from your blog, you'll want to ensure that you link the two together. Your website should list your LinkedIn profile URL anywhere that's appropriate.

Many websites are platforms intended to sell products and services. In these cases, it's better to drive traffic from LinkedIn to your site instead of the other way around. LinkedIn is used as a kind of funnel to get people to your website.

I recommend placing the URL of your LinkedIn page on your site's contact and about pages, as well as the footer of your posts. I recommend against including the link anywhere obvious, especially not above the fold (the upper part of the page which is visible without any scrolling.)

Using LinkedIn With Your Blog

Your blog, assuming it's different from your website, serves a different purpose. Blogs are more informative as their primary goal is to build relationships with customers and others who are interested in what you have to say as well as your products and services.

The purpose of your blog (to sell or to educate) will determine whether your blog prominently links to your LinkedIn profile or vice versa. The priority is always to get customers to purchase products and services; plan your linking strategy accordingly.

Regardless, include a link to your LinkedIn profile at the bottom of every post on your blog, as well as on the contact and about pages, plus any other pages which describe you, your company, services or brand.

Profile Badge

To help you promote your LinkedIn page, you can create a profile badge, which is a small graphic with a hyperlink to your LinkedIn page.

While logged into LinkedIn, visit the following link to see a list of all of the available profile badges, ready to copy and paste into your blog or website.

https://www.linkedin.com/profile/profile-badges

The badges are in HTML format which means you can copy it into a widget in WordPress or include the raw code on your site. Most social media platforms such as Facebook will not accept raw HTML code so you cannot use these badges there.

Company Page

"Your brand is that ADHESIVE image you carry, that has the ability to STICK to the minds of people you meet physically or otherwise. Brand yourself positively because whoever gets to know you when passing by takes your image along!" — **Israelmore Ayivor, Daily Drive 365**

While LinkedIn is primarily about branding individuals, you can create a company page which includes a brief summary and some links to your website and products or services.

Company pages on LinkedIn are simple and limited. You can enter a summary, a few links, a logo, an image, and a few brief notes about some of your products or services. LinkedIn doesn't offer much else for businesses.

Even so, go ahead and create a company page if it applies to your business. It's another way to attract people and to communicate your brand and message.

Keep in mind that the basis of LinkedIn is personal pages, i.e. people, and not businesses or companies. Thus, before you can create a Company page, you must have a personal LinkedIn profile.

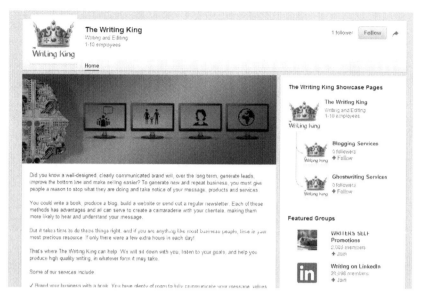

Exercise caution about where you define the Company page. For example, if you create one under the account of the receptionist, and she later quits or gets fired, you could lose access to the Company page. In this case, you'll have to re-create the page under someone else's profile. Not only will you lose control of that page, but you'll also lose the URL (it will change.)

CNAME for company page

You can make it easy to modify the address of your Company page by creating a subdomain. For example, suppose your website is example.com, and your LinkedIn company page is www.linkedin.com/company/example. Create a CNAME of company.example.com, which translates to the LinkedIn company name address of www.linkedin.com/company/example. Use the CNAME address on your website and anywhere else you refer to the Company page. If you have to move your

Company page to a new profile, thus changing the URL, all you have to do is change the CNAME instead of manually modifying every reference.

Creating a Company page is free, and you can create one or more whenever you want. Fill in all of the details, including the link to your website or blog, and some showcase entries for some of your products and services. Note that LinkedIn allows the creation of only two showcase pages each day.

Include a link to your Company page from your website, blog, and social networks. (Use the CNAME method described in the note above to make changes simpler.)

Regularly post status updates from your Company page to keep people informed about what's going on in your business. This is an excellent way to engage your customer base because you can provide them short articles about your company's products, services, and events as well as general information.

Showcase Pages

A Company page can include one or more Showcase pages, which are small web pages designed to show off a single product or services. You can create up to two of these each day, and each can include a short paragraph of text, URL, a logo and a graphic.

Group Strategies

Groups in LinkedIn work much the same way as groups in every other social networking platform. They are collections of individuals interested in discussing shared interests, common beliefs or an area of business.

Each group is intended to be a forum for discussions regarding a particular topic. For example, there might be a group about the subject of poetry and another about auto mechanics. The discussions within those groups are expected to be in some way related to the topic.

A group typically has one or more administrators who ensure that the posts remain faithful to the group topic and who also control spam. They also serve as gatekeepers, approving or denying membership, and occasionally banning people entirely.

Joining Groups

To improve your brand and attract people to your network, join groups consisting of members of your target audience. You can also join groups related to your profession, or a specific interest; remember, though, your purpose is to network with people who can help you, who will purchase your products or services, or who will make the decision about hiring you.

For example, I am a writer, so I tend to gravitate toward writing groups. It's useful to network with other authors, but these are not the decision makers who are going to purchase my services, although they may have ideas and leads that can be helpful. Writers usually don't buy ghostwriting or technical writing services.

My clientele is mid to high-level managers of corporations, up to and including the CEO. Higher level managers, especially those in the c-level, are more likely to have the funds as well as the need to have a book ghostwritten.

There are other markets for these services, including politicians, older people who want to write their memoirs, and even ministers. I make it a point to join several groups containing those people as well.

You should join as many groups as allowed, up to the one hundred permitted by LinkedIn. A good strategy, as indicated above, is to join a few made up of your peers or people who share your interests. Make sure you are a member of groups containing your target audience, and others containing, perhaps, consultants or vendors that you might find useful.

Validate that a group is active before joining. Look it over quickly to verify there have been posts in the last few days and that people are commenting on those posts.

Additionally, join groups that have a large number of members. While it's true that a small group occasionally can be beneficial, a large one will extend your network, and give you more chances for your message to be seen by others.

You don't have to keep your membership to groups static. You can leave and join groups at will. If you find a particular group isn't particularly useful, just leave it and find another one to join.

Why join as many groups as possible? Groups extend your network, meaning that anyone within your groups can communicate with you, and you can communicate with them. People outside your network require an InMail message, which costs money.

Thus, by being a member of well-chosen groups, you increase the size of your network by leaps and bounds. Not only that, but you dramatically enhance the value of your network.

Using Groups

Now that you're a member of some groups, it's time to start using them appropriately. Visit them occasionally, and quickly review a few of the most recent posts. Comment once in a while with something useful and appropriate. Don't spend a significant amount of time on this, but it's wise to find a few posts now and then and contribute.

I like to spend about an hour a week scanning a dozen of my groups for discussions where I can add value to the conversation. In these cases, I'll answer with a clarification or whatever is appropriate, keeping any sales talk out of the response.

Occasionally, 2 or 3 times a week, I'll post a question, a link to a useful article or an observation of some kind.

The idea is to build up your credibility with your target audiences. After doing this for some time, you'll begin to be known as a person who has the answers, who is willing to contribute, and who becomes an influencer.

As with all social networks, it can be a temptation to go overboard. Posting and groups can be very addictive as it can be very satisfying to be in communication with so many people. But remember that while this is reinforcing your brand and building your credibility — it is not directly generating income. An hour or two a week is the most that you should spend on these activities.

LinkedIn is not a sales platform. Refrain from making direct pitches of your products and services. It's considered bad form, and will tend to turn away people, which is the opposite effect from what you want. It could even get you banned from groups if you do it too much.

You should focus on being helpful, providing information, posting links to relevant information (not sales), answering and asking questions, and similar activities. These serve to build up your credibility and improve your branding, which in the long term can lead to sales of your products and services.

Signatures

Adding a short tag line to your posts and comments is acceptable on LinkedIn. For example, I include a single line to post which reads "Please feel free to connect with me."

Recommendations and Endorsements

Did you know that LinkedIn gives you two simple ways to improve your credibility? By giving and receiving recommendations, which are short paragraphs commending someone, you demonstrate your competence and leadership. Endorsements, because they are granted by others, strengthen the perception of your competence and skill.

For an optimal branding experience with LinkedIn, add both of these methods to your recurring LinkedIn tasks. Over time, these will give viewers of your profile a clear understanding of your strengths, competence and value.

Giving recommendations

Everyone has worked with people who help them in some way. In fact, I'm sure you can think of something positive to say about almost anyone, even if you had to think about it for a while.

A good way to thank those people is to give them a recommendation. These are short, usually 1 to 2 paragraphs long. The idea is to say something positive about their work performance or attitude or whatever comes to mind that will give others insight on the person.

Giving a recommendation is a nice thing to do. You can think of it as an acknowledgment of someone who has performed well or delivered a quality product or service.

You can give a recommendation to any connection, whether they work for you, you work for them, they were a customer, or you just met them yesterday while walking in the park. You just have to be connected to them on LinkedIn.

A salesperson could give recommendations to his clients, a manager might recommend subordinates and vice versa, and customers may recommend their consultants. The possibilities are endless and limited only by the number of people connected to you.

Since recommendations are short, they don't take much time to write. I've never spent more than five minutes putting one together.

When you write a recommendation, make a point to read it over a couple of times before you send it off to check for grammar and spelling errors. Remember, a poorly written recommendation makes you, the person who wrote it, look bad.

What should you write? Sometimes all you need to do is to note that they were easy to work with or did a good job on a big project. You might add they communicated well, knew how to handle meetings, and contributed to the team in a positive way.

For example:

Richard and I have worked together to help him promote two of his books: "Real World Survival Tips" and "Safe Computing is Like Safe Sex". He is professional and courteous and displays a wealth of knowledge and enthusiasm in his writing. I look forward to working with him again.

As you can see, short and to the point.

By giving recommendations, you will create goodwill and readers will gain a positive impression of you. Helping others can be a valuable part of your branding exercise as it builds a feeling of trust and camaraderie.

Another advantage of writing a recommendation is that it inserts a link to your profile in another person's profile on LinkedIn, which creates a different way for people to find you on the LinkedIn network.

For example, let's say I managed an applications developer named Shelley years ago. She found me on LinkedIn, and we connected, and since we had a good working relationship, I wrote a recommendation for her. From that point forward, when someone looks through Shelley's profile they will see my name and a link to my profile within her profile.

Ensure your recommendations are truthful and only give them to those who deserve praise for a job well done. Don't reinforce bad behavior by writing recommendations for people who didn't perform well, who delivered bad service, or who had a bad attitude.

Don't give negative recommendations. The recipient can easily refuse to accept them, and if they do allow it to be displayed it makes you look vindictive and petty.

Receiving recommendations

You can also receive recommendations from any of your connections. In fact, you can, and should, ask for them.

It's a good idea to make it a point to get several recommendations for at least your last three positions if possible. Just the fact of having received recommendations improves your credibility and solidifies your branding.

The most important recommendations are those from higher levels of management, as high up in the organization board as you can reach. Receiving a short recommendation from the CEO is far more impressive than getting recommendations from the people currently working for you.

Famous individuals or influencers who are well known to your niche or clientele are ideal candidates for recommendations. These are like gold and go a long way towards reinforcing your credibility.

Under "Privacy and Settings", click the link titled "Manage your recommendations." From there you'll be able to request, give, delete, and maintain recommendations.

When you're asking for a recommendation, a useful strategy is to create it for them. Just write up a few sentences and include them in your request.

Hi John, remember how we worked together on a big project a few years ago? I was wondering if you could recommend me; it would help. I would like to suggest the following, "I have been working with Richard for about 14+ years. Richard knows and understands technology. He is very open to learning more and hearing about all of the solutions out there that can help his organization be more productive and secure. He would be an asset to any organization!"

They might make a change or two, but you've made it very easy for them. All they need to do is cut and paste your words into the recommendation, modify a few words, and send it off.

Writing these yourself might seem presumptuous, but high-profile leaders are often extremely busy, and if you wait for them you may never get recommended. By suggesting the text for them, you show you value their time and increase your chances of their response.

Endorsements

Skills and Endorsements are LinkedIn's attempt to demonstrate your strengths to employers, potential clients, and vendors. Think of these as a way for a person to say they know you, and they agree that you are good at that skill. With one quick look at the Skills and Endorsements section, a viewer sees a summary of your strengths in one quick glance.

The ten skills of the top of the list are considered to be the most important ones. They are singled out and displayed separately, with the remainder ones shown in a single paragraph below them.

These endorsements show that some people took the time to click buttons indicating that, in their opinion, you're good at those skills. On the other hand, LinkedIn makes it so easy that the value of these endorsements is questionable.

It's a good idea to endorse people that you know, as it is an excellent way to acknowledge their abilities. By doing this, you help them by showing others that you agree with one or more of their strengths.

Fill in the Skills and Endorsements section entirely with fifty skills that apply. Spend the time to sort them so that your most important skills are at the top of the list and your least important are at the bottom.

Once you've done the work of entering your skills and sorting them into the proper order, don't spend a lot of time worrying about them. You'll find that as time goes by your connections will endorse you without any effort on your part.

Conclusions

Recommendations are a good way to improve your credibility and improve your brand. By giving them, you demonstrate that you have gratitude and a willingness to acknowledge others.

Receiving recommendations, especially from influencers or people much higher in the organization, adds credibility to the statements you make in your LinkedIn profile.

Both of these strategies are an essential part of your regular LinkedIn activities. I make it a point to give a couple of recommendations a week, and ask for one from a coworker or client regularly.

Additionally, spend the time to create a correctly sorted list of your skills, and you'll find that LinkedIn will do the work to get you endorsed as a matter of course. These can be useful in that they give others an idea of the skills you possess with a simple, quick glance.

Offline Marketing with LinkedIn

LinkedIn is also valuable for your off-line marketing and branding efforts. Print your *LinkedIn URL* on various marketing and advertising literature and publications. By including your URL, you make it easy for your customers and vendors to connect with you on LinkedIn.

Business cards

Add your LinkedIn URL to your cards. The back of the card is a good place for it since it is usually empty of content. Doing this ensures that everyone who receives your card has your LinkedIn address and an invitation to connect.

Connect with me on LinkedIn
https://www.linkedin.com/in/richardlowejr

Put the usual information on the front of the card, such as your business name, address, phone number, and website address.

Letterhead

Include your LinkedIn URL on your letterhead. Adding the URL to the bottom of the page, perhaps below your other contact information, is a good place to put this information. Every letter that you send out using your letterhead will implicitly invite the receiver to connect with you and thereby will increase the size of your network.

The Writing King • 340 S. Lemon Ave Suite 5029, Walnut, CA 91789 • 727.475.1283

www.thewritingking.com • rich@thewritingking.com
https://www.linkedin.com/in/richardlowejr

Conferences

If you're speaking at a conference, a networking group or anywhere else, ensure your materials include the URL of your LinkedIn profile.

Also, post on LinkedIn any white papers, notes, videos or any other documents from or about your talk. Use the various media links under your experiences, education, and summary.

Add a note to the last page of your presentation slides (PowerPoint) to let everyone know that your materials will be available for download on LinkedIn. You can use an account on a service called *SlideShare* to post those presentations.

Attending Events

People visit many different kinds of events during their professional career. These include classes, trade shows, networking events, colleges, seminars, and others. One thing all of these events have in common is the ritual known as the exchange of business cards.

It goes like this: you meet someone at an event and shake their hand. Each of you reaches for your card, and you hand them to each other. You shove that business card in your pocket, intending to reference it later. Sometimes you follow-up, and sometimes you don't.

It's a good idea to get in the habit of going through those stacks of business cards, sending a connection request to each person. Include a note in the message reminding them that you met at that event so they don't mark it as spam.

You can delegate this task to your secretary or even outsource to a virtual assistant for a few dollars. It's well worth the effort, as this will grow your network and make it easier to follow up and communicate.

Media

To make your LinkedIn profile stand out and get noticed, add photographs, videos, slideshows or other media. By doing this, you add pizazz to your profile, showcase your brand, and leverage the power of multimedia and images.

You can add media to your summary, each of your experiences, and each education section.

 Experience

Ambassador - Tampa and Clearwater
Doctor Pocket
January 2016 – Present (1 month) | Montreal, Quebec Canada

Imagine having a doctor in your pocket! Well, in today's world of high speed internet, ubiquitous wireless access and smart phones, the dream can become reality. Doctor Pocket, soon to be launched, is an application for smartphones which allows anyone to get medical advice (of a non-emergency nature) directly from a doctor anywhere on the globe.

I was brought on to produce weekly articles to help promote and market this incredible and useful service.

Doctor Pocket PROMO

When someone visits your page and clicks on that image, LinkedIn displays a popup where your visitor can view the media (video, presentation or whatever) and get more information about your brand, products, services or whatever else you want to communicate.

For documents, images (photos) and presentations you may either directly upload them to LinkedIn or specify their URL.

To add media, edit your profile and then navigate down to the experience, school or summary. Find the line that starts with "Add Media:" and click the button for the appropriate type of item.

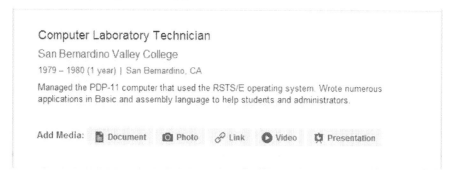

If the line does not exist in the experience, summary or school, go to another one and use that line instead. Once you press the button for the type of media, you will be prompted "Add to Position". Use the drop-down list to insert the media into the appropriate position.

Using Media to Improve Your brand

Adding photos, illustrations, slideshows, videos and other media to your LinkedIn profile can dramatically improve the engagement from visitors. The written word is a good way to get across ideas and information, but a well-placed photo, an excellent video or an informative slideshow causes people to stop and take a look.

Images and Photos

Ensure any images directly relate to the section of your profile in which they appear. For example, an engineer might include a picture of the computer that he designed; the manager of a transoceanic shipping company could include pictures of ships, cranes, and the front office; and a hotel executive might include an image of the top rated hotel in the chain.

Use photos or illustrations that reinforce the message that you are trying to portray. Ensure that your photos are professional, or at least very well done, with good lighting and a sharp focus.

Avoid photos that are overly personal in nature. Topics such as family, girlfriends, significant others, weddings (unless that is your business), and such belong on Facebook, not LinkedIn.

Documents

Include a few documents to reinforce or illustrate points, skills, or projects. For example, you can add white papers, articles, a chapter of a book you've written, a reference letter, or any other types of documents.

Avoid attaching your resume to your LinkedIn profile. It's far better to have potential employers, customers and others contact you directly for more information. Resumes are often used to eliminate candidates, and they can contain much information that is personal and should not be online for the public to see.

Videos

One of the best ways that you can add credibility to your profile and demonstrate your knowledge or skills in an area is to include a video. YouTube videos are great for this purpose.

Make sure your videos are well produced, although not necessarily professional, and show off your subject at its best. Remember, the point is to make you look good, and a poorly produced video can have the opposite effect.

Authors can create video trailers of their books, dancers might link to music videos, and the executive of a hotel could include a video showcasing the highlights of the chain. There are many tools available to produce short animated clips, and these can be very useful for explaining things. Applications such as CrazyTalk and CrazyTalk Animator are perfect for creating short animated clips, very helpful for communicating ideas. They also look great.

Presentations

A presentation is an excellent way to explain a product or demonstrate a service. A presentation can be in PDF or one of several different PowerPoint formats, and you can link to them on the web or upload them directly into your profile.

Using *SlideShare*, you can create dynamic presentations which include audio, video, and images to make your point. These are very simple to build and maintain and they look gorgeous.

Links

Sometimes it's best to link directly to a webpage, rather than to try to fit it into one of the categories of media. Do this, for example, if you want to link to a storefront, an order page, your website or your blog. Sometimes authors and marketers use the media type of URL to promote their product or something they're giving away for free.

Network Building Strategies

There are several schools of thought on how to build a network on LinkedIn. Some espouse that you should accept connections from anyone and everyone to build your network as large as possible. Others handpick each connection to ensure that they are a good fit for their efforts. And of course, there are variations on both of the strategies.

Willy nilly Networks

The majority of users on LinkedIn don't put much thought into the building of their networks. They accept connection requests from people they know or respect, rarely reach out to connect with others and put no thought or planning into the process.

Building up your connections using this approach doesn't fully leverage LinkedIn and its benefits. Haphazardly built networks don't add much value since they are random sets of people with little engagement. Getting these people to be involved can take more work than those in a carefully built network since there is little in common between you and them.

The majority of LinkedIn users tend to have relatively few connections, far less than five hundred. They may have as few as a dozen or as many as a couple of hundred. They don't spend much time on LinkedIn; they have minimal information in their profiles, and their engagement is limited.

Hand Built Networks

Some LinkedIn members are very choosy about whom they add to their network. Their concept is to build strong relationships with every connection and use LinkedIn to help with that process.

These members will reject a connection request from people they don't know or those who have no bearing in their field or area of expertise. They have small networks – usually less than five hundred individuals – since they want to make sure that every single person is known, engaged and provides some value.

LIONs

On the other end of the spectrum are the LIONs, whose purpose is to build LinkedIn networks as large and as quickly as possible. LION stands for LinkedIn Open Networkers, and they will accept a connection request from just about anyone. Many of them have the word LION as part of their heading or embedded in their summary.

LIONs aggressively build their networks, sending out connection requests regularly, and noting in groups and elsewhere that they are soliciting connections. Many of them take great pride in the number of people they have in their network, sometimes citing quantities of twenty or thirty thousand connections, and occasionally even more.

Many LIONs build large groups for the sake of building an extensive network. You could call them collectors of connections. The value of joining their networks is to be able to network with their connections.

Some LIONs aggressively sell or market to their connections, even to the point of spamming. Spamming is annoying, and when it happens you can disconnect from their network if you want.

What is a good strategy?

Your connecting strategy depends on your goals for LinkedIn. Salespeople may want to build large, extensive networks on the theory that the more people there are; the more potential sales exist. On the other hand, a manager who has been in the same position for twenty years may want to build a smaller, carefully cultivated network.

I don't recommend actively seeking out massive numbers of people to add to your network. It's a lot of work that can be better put into other marketing efforts or into actually making money.

On the other hand, a strict policy of only adding familiar or helpful people to a network doesn't take the best advantage of LinkedIn's branding capabilities. One of the concepts of networking is to connect with people even if they are not immediately helpful; they may know others who can be of value.

Conclusions

The strategy you choose for building your network depends on your brand, your purpose, and your personal approach. Larger networks allow open communication between more people, but when they get too large, they become unmanageable and often are used for spamming purposes. Make the choice that suits your needs, and be willing to change as your needs and knowledge change.

LinkedIn Spam

It should come as no surprise that LinkedIn has its share of spam, just like everything else on the Internet. The good news is that LinkedIn does a better job of controlling spam than most of the other social networks.

Some of the things you need to look out for are false profiles, spamming connection requests, spam messages, and spamming into groups.

False Profiles

Every once in a while you run across a profile on LinkedIn that doesn't look right. The profile may not have much information, there may only be a few connections, or the profile picture might appear strangely out of place.

Scammers create false profiles so that they can perform a little social engineering. Sometimes these are Advanced Fee Scams, (also known as the 419 or the Nigerian scam), and sometimes they are hackers or even extortionists trying to get their hooks into you. In my experience, LinkedIn is pretty good at spotting these and deleting them pretty quickly.

Any profile that has little information is pretty easy to spot as fake or false. Of course, people who are new to LinkedIn often have very thin profiles as well, but if you get a connection request from someone that you don't know whose profile is more or less empty, it's a pretty good bet that is false.

A profile picture that is out of place is a dead giveaway of a spammy profile. Scammers will use photos that they find off the Internet, and they are not very discreet about what they use. The photo almost certainly won't be a professionally done headshot.

Use a little discretion before connecting with random strangers. Make sure their profile, at least, looks real, and has some information that makes sense.

Scammers, for the most part, are in a hurry, and they tend to get chatty after connecting. The conversation can be strange, about things that have nothing to do with work. In one instance, a scammer asked me to wire her several thousand dollars because she was trapped at an airport overseas without any money. I had just met her in California the day before, so I knew she was not in London, which made the scam pretty obvious.

Use the block function liberally, and report them to LinkedIn. There is no value in communicating with scammers.

Spamming Connection Requests

LinkedIn frowns upon sending connection requests to people you don't know or who don't know you. This rule introduces a mild catch-22, in that you have to talk to someone to connect, but you can't easily communicate with them without connecting.

There are several ways around this conundrum. You could just send the connection request; most of the time the recipient will accept, or, at worst, delete it. But you are taking a chance of getting reported for spam.

If there is an email address or website listed in their profile, you can send a message directly to the person asking them to connect.

LinkedIn will allow you to send a message, known as an InMail, to anyone within or outside of your network. There is no charge to send an InMail to someone in your network (including your groups); however, to send to someone outside it will cost you $10 per message.

You can ask someone to introduce you to the person. This approach can be very successful, but it does add a few extra steps to the process.

I've found it is a good strategy to end every post, every status update, and every comment with the statement "Please connect with me." Doing this causes people to connect with YOU, which prevents anyone from reporting you for sending spammy connections.

LinkedIn is Not Facebook

Facebook is the largest social network on the planet with literally billions of users. It is unimaginable how significant this networking platform has become, and it still growing and getting bigger by the day.

LinkedIn is not Facebook (or Google+, or similar social networks.) These networks have entirely different purposes and audiences. Facebook tends to be used for just about everything, connecting families and friends across the whole planet. People post anything from pictures of their pets to their political rants to their sexual preferences on a regular basis.

On the other hand, LinkedIn is intended to be a place for business professionals to network and communicate with each other easily and quickly. It is a professional network; Save your personal postings, political rants, jokes and so forth to Facebook or Google+.

Don't post math problems, videos of your pets, your sexual preferences or practices, unprofessional memes, pictures of the food that you are eating, political commentary, and anything else along those lines to LinkedIn. Keep it professional and related to business.

The whole idea of LinkedIn is to present individuals in the most professional manner possible so that others will want to network with them, hire them, or investigate their products and services.

In other words, the concept is to create a personal brand for your professional life. It's important to present yourself as competent, experienced, qualified and skilled at your job. Conversely, ensure that you don't put anything online, especially on LinkedIn, that makes you look incompetent, inexperienced and unqualified. Anything that shows you in a negative light is inappropriate for LinkedIn.

Maintain a professional profile, which doesn't mean it shouldn't be fun or lighthearted. Just don't add anything that you wouldn't want a prospect, potential employer, partner, vendor, employee or industry leader to see.

Mistaking LinkedIn for Facebook will detract from your personal brand and make it appear that you are undependable, incompetent or ignorant.

Multiple Profiles

Every once in a while, someone asks if they can create two different profiles for reasons which sound perfectly logical. This not allowed according to the LinkedIn EUA (End User Agreement). In fact, if LinkedIn finds out, they may delete one (or even both) profiles. It's not worth the risk.

Why would anyone want to have two profiles?

Let's say you had two different professions, perhaps you work as an engineer at one company and have a second job as the night watchman. Creating two profiles, one for each role, might seem to be the ideal solution. You can't do this according to LinkedIn's terms and conditions.

Another reason is you might want to look for a job on LinkedIn but not want your boss to know about it. Creating a second profile, under an assumed name, might seem like the perfect solution, except LinkedIn requires you to use your real name.

On occasion, the desire is to create a more personal LinkedIn profile and a second one that about your company. The proper way to do this is to create a company profile for your business and your personal profile about yourself.

The long and short of it is you can't have more than one profile under any conditions.

If you're looking for a job, and you don't want your boss to find out what's your LinkedIn profile, then you need to ensure your profile doesn't give it away.

How can you promote yourself in different ways without creating multiple profiles? One method is to create multiple experiences and projects that focus on the various aspects of your career.

For example, if you're an author, a public speaker, and a photographer, you could create three different "companies", and define an Experience entry for each one. Show each experience with a beginning year going through the present, and use it to write up a description of that particular position.

In the example above, you might create three experiences named "Public Speaker", "Photographer", and "Professional Author." Using this method, you have plenty of space to write up each of your separate careers. Your summary could then be written to tie those three "jobs" together.

Conclusion

LinkedIn is an excellent professional social networking tool. Using it correctly, you can attract like-minded professionals and build new business, get employed, and generate a positive impression of you and your abilities and skills.

Your professional brand on LinkedIn starts with your profile, and everything you include should define and reinforce your professional brand. To do that, before you start you must understand what message about yourself you are trying to communicate with the world.

Everything else in the profile, from your headline and photo all the way down to your volunteer activities, publications and certifications should quantify your message. Anything that doesn't support your professional brand in some way should be removed or toned down so as not to distract from your overall goal.

Branding is not a passive activity; you can't just define your profile and then go off and do other things and expect good results. You have to put effort into maintaining your profile, as well as your other branding activities such as your blog and website, on a regular basis.

You should spend some time each week updating your status, posting a brief article, sharing a web page or two, and contributing to groups. Since life is always changing, you should also regularly make modifications to your profile itself.

Attend classes, get certified, volunteer your time to charities, and then note these things on your LinkedIn profile. As you go through your professional life and your job changes, update your experience so that it reflects your current status.

By keeping your LinkedIn up-to-date, the search engines such as Google and LinkedIn search remain interested and will rank you higher, which makes you easier to find.

It seems like a lot of work, but if you forgo watching one or two television shows a week, that will give you the time you need to keep LinkedIn up-to-date. Thirty minutes to a couple of hours each week is more than enough time to stay on top of things.

Just as important, expand your network. As you meet new people in real life, add them to your LinkedIn connections. When you find yourself in a discussion with several individuals in a group, invite them to join your network. Don't forget to ask people that you know from Facebook, your contact list, Twitter, and other social networks as well.

By constantly changing and adding to your online LinkedIn presence, and in expanding your network, you will find, over time, more and more people will find your profile on their own and want to do business with you.

The process is gradual, but give it enough time and energy, and you will find yourself being highly rewarded.

Before you go

If you scroll to the last page in this eBook, you will have the opportunity to leave feedback and share the book with Before You Go. I'd be grateful if you turned to the last page and shared the book.

Also, if you have time, please *leave a review on Amazon*. Positive reviews are incredibly useful. If you didn't like the book, please email me at *rich@thewritingking.com* and I'd be happy to get your input.

About the Author

https://www.linkedin.com/in/richardlowejr
Feel free to send a connection request

Follow me on Twitter: @richardlowejr

Richard Lowe has leveraged more than 35 years of experience as a Senior Computer Manager and Designer at four companies into that of a bestselling author, blogger, ghostwriter, and public speaker. He has written hundreds of articles for blogs and ghostwritten more than a dozen books and has published manuscripts about computers, the Internet, surviving disasters, management, and human rights. He is currently working on a ten-volume science fiction series – the Peacekeeper Series – to be published at the rate of three volumes per year, beginning in 2016.

Richard started in the field of Information Technology, first as the Vice President of Consulting at Software Techniques, Inc. Because he craved action, after six years he moved on to work for two companies at the same time: he was the Vice President of Consulting at Beck Computer Systems and the Senior Designer at BIF Accutel. In January 1994, Richard found a home at Trader Joe's as the Director of Technical Services and Computer Operations. He remained with that incredible company for almost 20 years before taking an early retirement to begin a new life as a professional writer. He is currently the CEO of *The Writing King*, a company that provides all forms of writing services, the owner of *The EBay King*, and a Senior Branding Expert for *LinkedIn Makeover*. You can find a current list of all books on his *Author Page* and take a look at his exclusive line of coloring books at *The Coloring King*.

Richard has a quirky sense of humor and has found that life is full of joy and wonder. As he puts it, "This little ball of rock, mud, and water we call Earth is an incredible place, with many secrets to discover. Beings fill our corner of the universe, and some are happy, and others are sad, but each has their unique story to tell."

His philosophy is to take life with a light heart, and he approaches each day as a new source of happiness. Evil is ignored, discarded, or defeated; good is helped, enriched, and fulfilled. One of his primary interests is to educate people about their *human rights* and assist them to learn how to be *happy in life.*

Richard spent many *happy days* hiking in national parks, crawling over boulders, and peering at Indian pictographs. He toured the Channel Islands off Santa Barbara and stared in fascination at wasps building their homes in Anza-Borrego. One of his joys is *photography*, and he has photographed more than 1,200 belly dancing events, as well as dozens of Renaissance fairs all over the country.

Because writing is his passion, Richard remains incredibly creative and prolific; each day he writes between 5,000 and 10,000 words, diligently using language to bring life to the world so that others may learn and be entertained.

Richard is the CEO of The Writing King, which specializes in fulfilling any writing need. You can find out more at *https://www.thewritingking.com/*, and emails are welcome at *rich@thewritingking.com*

Books by Richard G Lowe Jr.

Business Professional Series

Business Professional Series

On the Professional Code of Ethics and Business Conduct in the Workplace – Professional Ethics: 100 Tips to Improve Your Professional Life - have you ever wondered what it takes to be successful in the professional world? This book gives you some tips that will improve your job and your career.

Help! My Boss is Whacko! - How to Deal with a Hostile Work Environment - sometimes the problem is the boss. There are all kinds of managers, some competent, some incompetent, and others just plain whacked. This book will help you understand and handle those different types of managers.

Help! I've Lost My Job: Tips on What to do When You're Unexpectedly Unemployed – suddenly having to leave your job can be a harsh and emotional time in your life. Learn some of the things that you need to consider and handle if this happens to you.

Help! My Job Sucks Insider Tips on Making Your Job More Satisfying and Improving Your Career – sometimes conditions conspire to make the regular trek to a job feel like a trip through Dante's Inferno. Sometimes, these are out of our control, such as a malicious manager or incompetent colleague. On the other hand, we can take control of our lives and workplace and improve our situation. Get this book to learn what you can do when your job sucks.

How to Manage a Consulting Project: Make money, get your project done on time, and get referred again and again – I found that being a consultant is a great way to earn a living. Managing a consulting project can be a challenge. This book contains some tips to help you so you can deliver a better product or service to your customers.

How to be a Good Manager and Supervisor, and How to Delegate – Lessons Learned from the Trenches: Insider Secrets for Managers and Supervisors – I've been a manager for over thirty years I learned many things about how to get the job done and deliver quality service. The information in this book will help you manage your projects to a high level of quality.

Focus on LinkedIn – Learn how to create a LinkedIn profile and to network effectively using the #1 business social media site.

Home Computer Security Series

Safe Computing is Like Safe Sex: You have to practice it to avoid infection – Security expert and Computer Executive, Richard Lowe, presents the simple steps you can take to protect your computer, photos and information from evil doers and viruses. Using easy-to-understand examples and simple explanations, Lowe explains why hackers want your system, what they do with your information, and what you can do to keep them at bay. Lowe answers the question: how to you keep yourself say in the wild west of the internet.

Disaster Preparation and Survival Series

Real World Survival Tips and Survival Guide: Preparing for and Surviving Disasters with Survival Skills – CERT (Civilian Emergency Response Team) trained and Disaster Recovery Specialist, Richard Lowe, lays out how to make you, your family, and your friends ready for any disaster, large or small. Based upon specialized training, interviews with experts and personal experience, Lowe answers the big question: what is the secret to improving the odds of survival even after a big disaster?

Creating a Bug Out Bag to Save Your Life: What you need to pack for emergency evacuations - When you are ordered to evacuate—or leave of your free will— you probably won't have a lot of time to gather your belongings and the things you'll need. You may have just a few minutes to get out of your home. The best preparation for evacuation is to create what is called a bug out bag. These are also known as go-bags, as in, "grab it and go!"

Professional Freelance Writer Series

How to Operate a Freelance Writing Business, and How to be a Ghostwriter – Proven Tips and Tricks Every Author Needs to Know about Freelance Writing: Insider Secrets from a Professional Ghostwriter – This book explains how to be a ghostwriter, and gives tips on everything from finding customers to creating a statement of work to delivering your final product.

How to Write a Blog That Sells and How to Make Money From Blogging: Insider Secrets from a

Professional Blogger: Proven Tips and Tricks Every Blogger Needs to Know to Make Money – There is an art to writing an article that prompts the reader to make a decision to do something. That's the narrow focus of this book. You will learn how to create an article that gets a reader interested, entices them, informs them, and causes them to make a decision when they reach the end.

Other Books by Richard Lowe Jr

How to Be Friends with Women: How to Surround Yourself with Beautiful Women without Being Sleazy – I am a photographer and frequently find myself surrounded by some of the most beautiful women in the world. This book explains how men can attract women and keep them as friends, which can often lead to real, fulfilling relationships.

How to Throw Parties like a Professional: Tips to Help You Succeed with Putting on a Party Event – Many of us have put on parties, and I know it can be a daunting and confusing experience. In this book, I share what I learned from hosting small house parties to shows and events.

Additional Resources

Is your career important to you? Find out how to move your career in any direction you desire, improve your long-term livelihood, and be prepared for any eventuality. Visit the page below to sign up to receive valuable tips via email, and to get a free eBook about how to optimize your LinkedIn profile.

http://list.thewritingking.com/

I've written and published many books on a variety of subjects. They are all listed on the following page.

https://www.thewritingking.com/books/

On that site, I also publish articles about business, writing, and other subjects. You can visit by clicking the following link:

https://www.thewritingking.com

To find out more about me or my photography, you can visit these sites:

Personal website: *https://www.richardlowe.com*
Photography: *http://www.richardlowejr.com*
LinkedIn Profile: *https://www.linkedin.com/in/richardlowejr*
Twitter: *https://twitter.com/richardlowejr*

If you have any comments about this book, feel free to email me at *rich@thewritingking.com*

Premium Writing Services

Do you have a story that needs to be told? Have you been trying to write a book for ages but never can seem to find the time to get it done? Do you want to brand your business, but don't know how to get started?

The Writing King has the answer. We can help you with any of your writing needs.

Ghostwriting. We can write your book, which entails interviewing you to get your story, writing the book and then working with you to revise it until complete. To discuss your book, contact *The Writing King* today.

Website Copy. Many businesses include the text on their sites as an afterthought, and that can result in lost sales and leads. Hire *The Writing King* to review your site and recommend changes to the text which will help communicate your message and improve your sales.

Blogging. Build engagement with your customers by hiring us to write a weekly or semi-weekly article for your blog, LinkedIn or other social media. Contact *The Writing King* today to discuss your blogging needs.

LinkedIn. LinkedIn is of the most important vehicles for finding new business, and a professionally written profile works to pulling in those leads. *Write or update your profile* today.

Technical Writing. We have broad experience in the computer, warehousing and retail industries, and have written hundreds of technical documents. Contact *The Writing King* today to find out how we can help you with your technical writing project.

The Writing King has the skills and knowledge to help you with any of your writing needs. Call us today to discuss how we can help you.

Index

Index

resumes · 4

S

Scammers · 103
search engine listings · 9
Search engines · 63
selfies · 26
SEO · 44
Showcase pages · 74
signature · 64
skills · 5, 45
Skills and Endorsements · 46, 86
Skype · 42
SlideShare · 97
slideshows · 93
sloppy profile · 5
social media · 3
social networks · 7, 78
spam
    LinkedIn · 103
status updates · 60
strategy · 11
summary · 29

T

Twitter · 8, 9

U

URL · 40, 89

V

videos · 50, 93, 96
volunteer · 50

W

website · 9, 11, 67, 68
websites · 3
who has viewed your profile · 15
Wordle · 19
WordPress · 11

Made in the USA
San Bernardino, CA
03 January 2018